THE
ART
OF
WAR

D1043050

THE
ART
OF
WAR

*The Definitive Interpretation of
Sun Tzu's Classic Book of Strategy*

STEPHEN F. KAUFMAN
Hanshi 10th dan

TUTTLE Publishing

Tokyo | Rutland, Vermont | Singapore

Published by Tuttle Publishing, an imprint of Periplus Editions (HK) Ltd.

www.tuttlepublishing.com

Copyright © 1996 by Stephen F. Kaufman

All rights reserved. No part of this publication may be reproduced or utilized in any form or by any means, electronic or mechanical, including photocopying, recording, or by any information storage and retrieval system, without prior written permission from the publisher.

Library of Congress Cataloging-in-Publication Data

Kaufman, Steve, 1939-
   The art of war; the definitive interpretation of Sun Tzu's classic
   book of strategy for the martial artist / by Stephen F. Kaufman.
      xii, 109 p. ; 22 cm.
   I. Sun-Tzu, 6th cent. B.C. Sun tzu ping fa. 2. Military art and science—
   Early works to 1800. I. Sun-tzu, 6th cent. B.C. Sun-tzu ping fa.
   English. II. Title
UI0I.S96K38 1996
355.02.dc20

96001570
CIP

ISBN 978-0-8048-3080-5

Distributed by:

North America, Latin American & Europe
Tuttle Publishing
364 Innovation Drive
North Clarendon, VT 05759-9436 U.S.A.
Tel: I (802) 773-8930
Fax: I (802) 773-6993
info@tuttlepublishing.com
www.tuttlepublishing.com

Asia Pacific
Berkeley Books Pte. Ltd.
61 Tai Seng Avenue #02-12
Singapore 534167
Tel: (65) 6280-1330
Fax: (65) 6280-6290
inquiries@periplus.com.sg
www.periplus.com

Japan
Tuttle Publishing
Yaekari Building, 3rd Floor
5-4-12 Osaki
Shinagawa-ku
Tokyo 141 0032
Tel: (81) 3 5437-0171
Fax: (81) 3 5437-0755
sales@tuttle.co.jp
www.tuttle.co.jp

18 17 16 15   22 21 20 19 18 17 16
Printed in Singapore   1502MP

TUTTLE PUBLISHING ® is a registered trademark of Tuttle Publishing,
a division of Periplus Editions (HK) Ltd.

This book is dedicated to Lita,
Adam, Andrew (the newest warrior),
and to all the next generations in our clan.

CONTENTS

Introduction

Sun Tzu lived approximately two thousand years ago—if in fact he lived at all. In those times, generally, works like *The Art of War* were passed along by word of mouth by enlightened people and in time the lessons became corrupted. Taught in Sun Tzu's name, these lessons are fundamental for intelligent people who seek an understanding of conquest and the application of it, according to their own goals. In this work you will learn how people are to be treated and dealt with. The work was written for men in command and leaders of states. It is for the ambitious and strong spirited; do not seek morality lessons here.

Sun Tzu has been translated and interpreted countless times by people with little knowledge of true combat reality on either the physical or mental level. It has been called any number of things, but it still remains a guide for the control of people, places, and things. It can be construed as mortal-combat specific or as a general guide to management—aggressive, high-minded, goal-oriented management.

Most of the available translations and interpretations maintain a poetic approach that really doesn't pertain to the times we are living in. There is a tendency to maintain a "mystique" regarding ancient knowledge. This is quaint, relative to today's aggressive personality. We are living in a global network and must think in decisive terms if we are to succeed in our various business dealings—which can take place in a boardroom, a courtroom, a barroom, or the battlefield; wherever you may choose.

In this interpretation I detail the actions that must be taken to maintain control of an environment. Obviously, the explanations must be put into the context of the reader's experience. It is, therefore, a real-time book. My work is thoroughly grounded in experience and is the product of intense meditation on the precepts first suggested by Sun Tzu. A hard-nosed, cold-blooded mentality is essential to personal development both on the field of battle and at the negotiating table, and if you wish to succeed in such situations, you must act accordingly. This mentality is required if you truly desire to be one among the few.

I leave out the commentaries by alleged ancient masters as to what Sun Tzu supposedly meant. These commentaries were generally given as edifications by others so they could tell you their ideas. In reality, who cares what Ch'en Fu thinks about Sun Tzu's hidden meaning about the jade stalk in the midst of the enemy's goldfish pond? We are grown-up and intelligent enough to develop our own understanding without the need for quaint allegories. There is nothing sacred here. I find that approach unnecessary, limiting, and a waste of time to the educated reader. The only comments and clarifications you will ever need should be your own and they should be based on your understanding and application of the knowledge. You should take notes for your own personal needs.

Interpretations and translations of ancient works will come and go. Some will remain in force and others will fall by the wayside. It doesn't matter what happens to a work as long as that work is done with sincerity and a knowledge of the truth of the matter. The attitudes and ideas that I discuss require understanding and insight on the part of the reader. This book is a philosophy of management; it is not about how to change a lightbulb, although, in the final analysis, it could be. How you use the information is the only aspect of the work that should have any functional value for you. As a student, what you consider right or wrong, correct or incorrect, can only be determined by yourself.

A word about my selection of terms. I have selected the rank of "warlord" because I feel that it is this person who is generally in charge of the "campaign to maintain," regardless of gender or specific titles such as boss, president, king, etc. I preserve the identification of all involved in a masculine format. This is not to belittle women, and no offense is intended. However, the tenor of "war" is mostly of male "feather flashing," irrespective of the fact that I personally realize the superiority of women in many matters of leadership. The term "ruler" is generically used where perhaps "prince," "king," or "empress" could also have been used.

I leave it to you to judge the work on its own merits. If you follow the precepts laid out for you then you will see radical changes in the manner in which you conduct your life—on every level.

As an acknowledged and world-recognized martial arts master, a Hanshi (which is the highest rank attainable), I am thoroughly aware of my responsibility for the interpretation of this doctrine, and I have made it incumbent upon myself to explain Sun Tzu's tenets as I perceive them in a definitive manner.

THE
ART
OF
WAR

BOOK 1

CONSIDERATIONS AND
ESTIMATIONS FOR WAR

Conflict is essential to the development and growth of man and society. It leads either to the construction or destruction of an entire group or state. As a leader of men, you should understand this concept without question. If you do not understand the need for conflict, then you should not be in control of the society you presume yourself to be in charge of.

If there is no conflict—internal or external—there can be no growth. The resolution of a warlord's affairs, worldly or otherwise, forces personal development in the individual. However, conflict does not always mean physical combat. Being prepared for any eventuality by understanding the controls required to develop your own particular agenda are essential. You must see the need for battle if you wish to develop your own cause on any level, but you should not fight a battle if you cannot foresee winning the war.

The warlord, understanding the tools used to wage war, must also understand men and must have the presence of mind to give orders without hesitation, regardless of the outcome. This is essential. Correct preparations will generally insure a successfully carried out campaign.

The reality of life and the attitudes of the fates play an important role. You cannot know if you will be successful or not. You can only prepare for battle, and it must be done with all of your heart and with all of your consciousness. In that manner you will have the edge. Being unprepared will bring about defeat unless you are truly exceptional, and there are very few who fit that description. It is stupid to fight a battle that you cannot win, and you cannot win unless you have properly planned for it. Fate, which is based on your true desire, will determine the outcome of the conflict according to the extent of your own belief and faith: nothing more, nothing less.

The wrong weapons placed in the hands of untrained soldiers will result in defeat because of a lack of consideration given the matter by the leader. Generally, men know their own weapons and are comfortable with them. Choose your men with great care and consideration. To let fate choose your situation invites defeat. As a warlord you must be courageous. When you have chosen your men, keep them at your breast, nurture them, and care for them. They will not fail you under these conditions. Never betray them, regardless of your anger at their mistakes. They must know you will die in battle with them if it is required.

Think about the following ideas with deep resolve. Meditate with understanding. Preparation for war takes considerable study before orders should be passed to generals and then to the captains and ranks.

1) The morality of the project is essential to the outcome of the project. You must know what it is you wish to accomplish and why. Be firm in your resolve and certain that your generals and

captains agree with your desires and can be depended upon to
take the matter to the final point. Do they believe strongly
enough in your ideal to sacrifice everything that has to be sacri-
ficed for the accomplishment of the goal? Do they believe in you
as a leader? Do YOU believe in yourself as a leader? If everything
is balanced in your favor then proceed to the next step. If not,
rethink your attitudes and desires.

2) The atmosphere and the general attitude is most important.
Are the times correct, and can you properly prepare for battle?
Have you considered alternatives to the plan of operation? Can
you control the needs of your troops with regards to their suste-
nance? Can your supply lines be made secure? If you investigate
these matters and plan correctly, your troops will be secure in
your leadership and will not turn on you in mutinous fashion.

3) Are you capable of standing alone when necessary and making
decisions that will govern the outcome of the enterprise? Can you
penetrate with depth and escape at will? Is there room to renego-
tiate a situation (should it become necessary), in order to protect
the overall condition of your plan? If not, then you must rethink
the conditions and put them to your advantage. Once the war
begins someone must win and someone must lose, unless both
sides are insecure in their desires.

4) Do you have control over those who will wish to be in charge
when you have taken your new domain? Will those you delegate
authority to be able to deal with the new responsibilities thrust
upon them? Do your troops consider you to be compassionate
and strong, yet fair, humane, and truly concerned for their welfare? If they do not, then you will never be able to put your plans
into motion.

5) Will you do whatever is necessary to accomplish your goals, irrespective of the feelings of others who may otherwise wish you harm? You must be strong enough to confront those who will seek to pull you down. To accomplish your goals, you must consider the reactions of those you are not taking into consideration in your ultimate plan. Even if they believe in you, they will interfere because they know you are not keeping their well-being in mind. If you lie to them they will know that too. Their attempts at revenge will be sweet to them regardless of your success or failure.

6) The above matters taken into consideration, the warlord's general philosophy of the ideal must be made manifest before any physical action is taken. Are those to be deposed and reassigned able to maintain their dignity? Have you provided for their needs if you are unable to crush them resolutely? Are the enemy's men you are saving and delegating authority to able to deal with the changes they must come to terms with?

The successful warlord does not put someone in charge of the warehouse if that person only cares about negotiating. Everyone should be content with their given tasks and in that manner they will perform admirably. You must praise and admonish your men with the same intensity and you must never play favorites. Anything you do that is not built on balance will eventually topple, causing you great grief.

Treat all of your staff as equals and permit each member of your staff to know they are special in their place. But do not let them think they are equal to you. If they realize they are not your equal they will not try to assume command, thereby undermining your efforts. See that your staff treats their subordinates in the same fashion as you treat yours.

The ideas presented to you follow a sensible order, and one must not be considered more important than another. If you prefer one idea to another then you will not be in control of the situation. Trying to determine an easy way to accomplish your goals will, in time, cause you to be defeated. A warlord must maintain personal balance in all affairs.

A warlord of worth must consider all of these matters with an enlightened mind and at the same time maintain full authority and conviction of purpose. Do not let your men participate in your times of meditation. Their interruptions will interfere with your thoughts causing a loss of focus on your goals.

If these matters are given due consideration by one who is astute, then victory is practically assured, notwithstanding the fates. If you will think in these terms and come to understand them, then you will also know if the orders you give are within reason or if they are demands that you yourself would not dare follow.

A warlord must appear to be all things to all men, but first he must be true to himself and not permit indecisiveness to rule his destiny. There can be no room for indecision and nothing less than full commitment to the ideal. These principles must be grounded in his heart. It must be expressed through his actions towards his men: they will know if his affection is real or false and they will act accordingly.

If warriors under your command follow your instructions you will have great success. Reward them well and reward them equally, but not too often. If you feel otherwise, for whatever reason, or they give you cause to suspect that their true natures are not sympathetic to yours, they should be disposed of immediately and in proper fashion. If they cannot be trusted with you, then for certain they cannot be trusted among your enemies. If you permit them to remain in your presence, they might rush to the other side and reveal your plans when it is least expected. Do not take this chance. War does not permit faltering personal belief. Never seek to assuage the non-sympathetic in an attempt to convert them to your way of thinking. Empathy will be seen as a sign of weakness among your loyal followers. Men who do not follow instructions can never lead as commanders. They serve no purpose other than to use up valuable resources and create dissension. Dispose of them.

Compassion must be reserved for those who truly need it, and it must be offered with leniency, not indulgence. It debilitates and weakens the strong in their resolve to fight for you. Never try to win someone over by changing your strategy in hopes of befriending them. Hope is nothing more than wishful thinking and must be avoided at all costs: it abrogates definitive focus and creates false friends who are worse than true enemies. It also brings about flatterers. You must truly believe in your own ideal. Preparations for war cannot be intellectual exercises.

Once these principles are understood and they are taken into a warlord's heart, the next level of understanding can be approached—that of making war—without hesitation and without second thoughts.

Correct strategies must be developed by methods that

enable the warlord to bring about the implementation of his true beliefs. It does not matter how he does this. He must, however, make sure that his own house is protected before going into the field.

Going into the field means that all preparations are in place and effort can be minimized by using a primary tool of war—deception. The warlord must look busy doing something else when he is in fact positioning himself intelligently and with strength. Enemies must never see you in direct motion, such as coming at them. Enemies must never make sense of your actions.

In war it is essential to make the enemy think one thing while you deliver a strike from another direction. It is essential to keep the enemy off balance, even by feigning assistance to him. Make him think you are befriending him while you plan his demise.

Destroy your enemy in any way you can, but never forget that he may have resources as well and may be prepared for your attack. Consider him a fool for self-aggrandizement if it is appropriate, but do not become vain in your estimation of him nor permit yourself to consider him weak-minded, regardless of appearance. Remember, you did not invent war and he may be maintaining his place of power in the same manner that you maintain yours. Never think that he is incapable of destroying you.

If he moves right, you move right in an encircling gesture—leaving some men to move left. If he moves left, you move left in an encircling gesture—leaving some men to move right. Do not permit him to flank you. If he moves back, you move forward—leaving some men in the rear for support. If he moves in, you move in with greater resolve taking care to outflank him. All of your troops must be committed to the battle. They must be well equipped.

Insult the enemy with subtlety where and when you can insult him; degrade where and when you can degrade. Offer fool's bait and entice him to display his stupidity. Do something that may appear stupid and capitalize on his arrogance. Insult his children and insult his parents—it will anger him and bring about rash acts. Insult his wife—he physically joins with her and it will force him to focus his rage incorrectly. Insult him directly—as a commander he will be forced to protect his face and attack with less than well-thought-out tactics.

If he is not resolute in matters of war, he will easily be kept off guard. He will issue inappropriate orders, and his men will react without conviction and fall in battle. *It is always best to let the enemy kill himself.* If these actions do not motivate him towards combat, then you had best reconsider your enemy and his sense of beingness.

It is wise to keep the enemy on the move, forcing him to cover areas that ordinarily need no extended care. Create disturbances that force him to settle his mind elsewhere. Create dissension among his troops by providing them with gifts they would not ordinarily receive. Poison his food supplies. Disease his men with unclean women. Create a strain in his thinking and when he is flustered, drive in and destroy him—totally, including the people thought to be his allies who must be intimidated by your ferocity of purpose. If they were his allies, they cannot be your allies; at least in the present time. You will need time to watch them and see how they react to all of your actions and your enemy's defeat.

Do what I tell you to do. You will then always be successful in war. If you ask what happens if he does the same things to you, you do not understand what I am talking about. Study deeply.

BOOK 2

PREPARATIONS FOR WAR

Supplies are essential for the proper management of a conflict and its resolution. Without supplies there is nothing to sustain the army except bare hands and berries. Oversupply presents problems of a different nature. Though it may appear better to be oversupplied, consider the hindrance in mobility when approaching the enemy or when retreating.

Proper rationing of supplies includes food, ammunition, and money. All are equally important. Food is essential on the march: more so than weapons. Weapons are more important in combat than is food. Money is more important during times of rest. There must be adequate rationing of all supplies.

Without food the army cannot sustain its energy. Overfeeding troops will make them sluggish and interfere with their desire to win as much as too little food will make them nervous and edgy. There must be a sufficient supply of arrows and spears to replace those lost in battle and on the march. Replacements must be available when needed. Money must be paid when the troops are at rest. Some men may wish to buy presents for their loved ones. Some will prefer to gamble. Others will wish to buy books, trinkets, or sweets. The warlord should not be concerned with how a soldier spends his money, as long as it doesn't interfere with command.

All food, weapons, and money must be in safekeeping prior to ordering your troops into battle. Only then can you appropriately deploy your men. There should be enough money in reserve to counter any surprises that could deplete your supplies and force you to change your plans during unfavorable times.

The intelligent warlord understands that entrance into conflict is senseless without an attitude of complete and total victory. There is no reason to contemplate anything else. Paper tigers are burned up at the first contact with a flame and cease to exist. If victory is not his main goal, then what is to be accomplished? If plans do not include destruction of the enemy, the warlord's troops will sense this and develop a lack of morale. Their keenness for battle will be dampened by the lack of leadership, and they will challenge the chain of command. Neighboring states will also see that he has no heart for the matter and take pleasure in setting traps that they normally would not attempt. They will look to humiliate him and see him falter. He cannot permit these conditions to arise.

When mobility of troops is difficult and the enemy is more familiar with the territory, the edge in the battle will go to the enemy. Attacks must be delivered with blinding speed and proper plans must be well thought-out. If they are not, the enemy will detect the approach, giving him time to prepare his defenses. A lack of speed may be caused by not having been discriminate in selecting the correct fighting ground. An aware warlord knows that good ground is essential for the mobility of his troops. The place of fighting must be thoroughly researched before he can attack with authority. In this way he insures his victory, despite the unpredictability of fate.

A true understanding of the principles of war means that he does not need reinforcements to make the initial attack. If the attack is planned properly and the men are properly trained and prepared emotionally, mentally, and spiritually, the warlord will have investigated all possibilities.

Errors in judgment are not too rare and adequate force should be employed when attacking. This coupled with the speed of the attack comprises his action. If you determine that five hundred soldiers will do the job you must be sure to have a thousand. They must all travel together and understand the necessity of completing the maneuver in one thrust. They must have the heart to destroy the enemy. All provisions and supplies must be carried with the troops as they prepare to enter into battle. It is bad policy to have to call for supplies when involved with tactical maneuvers. Even worse is to discover that the supplies being requested are not available. This is poor planning and results in failure, unless Heaven is determined that you shall win the day.

It must also be realized that when the army is in the field, supplies are very expensive if they have to be locally procured. Peasants and usurers will charge as much as they can; that being the nature of peasants and usurers. An enlightened warlord knows that peasants do not really care who is in charge of the government; or for that matter who wins the conflict. They are only interested in providing for their families. It is a good idea to have them on your side and you should maintain their goodwill by giving them something extra. If they determine that you are weak in spirit or intent, they will take undue advantage and assist the very people you are attacking, whether they are in accord with them or not. If you are good to them, they will mind their own business. This does not mean that you are to trust them under any conditions. Regardless, when you subjugate them you don't have to trust them—they will fear you.

Taking what he needs from local peasants and merchants to replenish his troops, the warlord does not involve himself with commerce when he is in the midst of battle. He makes sure to leave some for the local people, knowing there is always the possibility that he will see them in a time of retreat. However, if the people deny assistance they should be destroyed. Peasants can be replaced: troops are not that easy to find. Although you may have adequate supplies in the rear, it takes some of those very supplies to deliver the remainder to the troops in the field.

Care must be taken not to humiliate the enemy troops more than is required for quick victory. The more humiliation you place on the enemy, the more vengeance he will crave, and the more intense his actions will be. If you intend to subjugate the enemy, do so within the constraints of intelligent planning for the future. There will be ramifications regardless of the manner in which you operate. Understand this before you make your final decision to overrun a country. If you see no value to the enemy in any way or fashion, then you should totally destroy every remnant of his culture. However, this is generally not wise because there is always something of value to be gained from other cultures. Change brings about change, though this is not always good.

Reward the warriors who have served with distinction to the maximum extent you can. Do not skimp on the rewards you place before them, and make sure to do so within the view of the other troops. Do not reward those who have done a halfhearted job, regardless of how fervent their halfheartedness was. Levy swift punishment to those who have created difficulty in your process of victory. Do that in front of the troops as well.

Concerning the warriors of the enemy that have not fallen before you: treat them with respect, especially if they have fought with all of their hearts. They can be made into allies and will serve you with great zeal if they learn respect for you. It does not matter that they have fallen. Perhaps their leaders were not as good as they thought they were and did not plan adequately. Perhaps their leaders demanded too much of them. The reasons are countless and you can do nothing to enhance your understanding of victory in war by pondering another's reasons for failure. You must carefully analyze the actions that brought you victory and, in that manner, determine where the enemy was weak.

Ever so intelligently, and with compassion, bring the enemy warriors into your own fold. But do not bunch them together; they can rise up against you when they realize what has happened. That is why it is well to reward the warriors of the enemy that have given great battle. Warriors are warriors and do not concern themselves with anything less than war. Do not humiliate them in their defeat. Do not deride their past masters more than is necessary to assert control for the benefit of all concerned.

If war is waged it must be for the benefit of all. This includes the people of the beaten country as well. If this attitude is not understood and prevalent then perhaps you are just a barbarian. If so, you will eventually fall. Do not think that because you have won in combat that you are invincible. The strength of your victory also depends on the weakness of your enemy, which you must have determined. After victory is attained, be prepared to govern the conquered. The people will do your bidding once you have their trust and if they believe you have done for them as you have done for your own people.

BOOK 3

THE NATURE OF ATTACKS

U nless it is absolutely necessary, never use force when taking control of another state. Not using force will enable you to relax the fears of the people. When they realize the meaning of your intentions, they will follow your lead and obey if you have properly prepared. If they are approached with respect, and the inevitability of your action is understood, they will seek to assist you as a means of protecting their own interests. They will be outwardly unafraid. Inwardly they will tremble.

When the enemy's army has been made impotent by this method, the wise warlord will show them the futility of attempting to engage in physical battle. It is best to have the enemy army align with you, making your takeover that much easier. Their masters will readily submit to you when their resources have deserted them.

Killing is always easier, but it is also the most costly in terms of manpower and the time required to reorganize the conquered people. Being perceptive, the warlord knows that a good deal of hatred has been created. The peasantry may have lost members of their own clans and may one day seek to destroy you. It is important, therefore, to blend the enemy troops in with your own before they realize they have become part of your army, thereby making it very difficult for their leaders to do anything about it. They should not be permitted to gather in numbers and must be widely dispersed among your own men.

In the order of Heaven it is best to attack in the following manner. The first way should be the total disruption of the enemy's intended plans for his future growth and success. When he sees that everything he is trying to do is blocked, and is unable to determine the place from where it is coming, he will be weakened. The enemy troops will think their leader is losing control of the natural order of things. They will be shy and act with great resistance when told to perform certain actions. This will cause great confusion in his ranks. It will serve you well if you understand the way to do these things and you should deeply meditate upon them. The ability to take control is made easier if care and planning for your own future is considered beforehand.

If you find that you are unable to disrupt his philosophy, the next best thing is to disrupt his alliances with other countries. This is done with educated subterfuge and outright lying. Starting rumors and placing blame properly for things that do not necessarily exist can bring about dynamic results if they are executed correctly with malice aforethought.

People will always have a desire to see the demise of any leader, including their own, if there is the slightest annoyance or inconvenience brought about by or because of that leader. People are generally unsteady when under pressure and they will usually follow the bread wagon and do so with little regard for future consequences. The masses of people are only concerned with their own welfare. That is why they are peasants and not leaders.

Warlords see the future; peasants only see the present, and grumblers only see the past. Whenever possible, use the grumblers to activate the peasants into overthrowing the leader's plans for the future. Create disturbances where you can and constantly force the blame into places of innocence by means of rumor and deceit. Usually, the innocent are not that innocent and are predisposed to being picked upon.

If the enemy is not strong and his government is not resolute, he will be unable to stop you. If the enemy sees what you are doing and begins to act against you, physically attack his army without hesitation. Perhaps you have not been correct under Heaven to carry out your well-meant but improperly conceived plans. You may have failed to adequately examine conditions for a nonviolent takeover. You must therefore destroy the army at what might be a great cost to you. The failure of your previous plans will make it imperative that you make the attack if you do not wish to lose face among your own people and lose your power. Your army should have been prepared for this eventuality, so it should not be that difficult to field it.

By being unsuccessful you have forewarned the enemy, and by being unable to take over with the previous methods you may have inspired their anger. They will now fight with more conviction to stop you, and your troops will suffer losses regardless of your apparent strength. You must attack with ferocity and fanatical enthusiasm if you are to succeed. You will have to convince your troops that the enemy has been unreasonable, and therefore must be stopped at any cost. This is called propaganda.

It does not matter that you may appear to be able to overwhelm the enemy. You must still be prepared and your generals must understand and believe your plans will succeed. You must be sure the generals are sympathetic to your thinking or you will suffer their ambivalence. If their hearts and minds are not with you, they will not be authoritative when they pass your orders to their captains.

In like manner you must maintain a patriotic mentality on all levels of negotiations with the enemy. Your plans are better for the enemy than his are for himself, and he must be made to see this, and he will if you have adequately approached his advisors. Your personal belief must be strong enough for his generals to understand and believe your intent. These truths must be in place if you are to avoid a physical war, which might come about later but not if you have effectively weakened his troops.

It is essential to fight in open areas without being caught up in the enemy's territory (which you can never know as well as he does). If you are unsuccessful in defeating the enemy armies in the field, and you think that you will be better able to bring him down by attacking his cities, you are incorrect. If you attack his cities—the most dangerous place to do battle—you will also be attacking the common folk, and they will rise up to defend their homes at any cost. This makes it more difficult for your troops to fight, and you will suffer additional losses because of guerrilla tactics.

If you don't plan properly for the disruption of the enemy's strategy then, more than likely, you didn't plan well for the disruption of his alliances either. The battle in the fields may not have been planned properly either, and you may find yourself fighting on his ground without a full understanding of the means to your own ends. If you do take the city, you will pay heavily and will have to reward your generals and troops that much more in order for them to remain loyal since you have shown that you were not capable in the first instance. You are now is a position to be overthrown by your own people who may enlist the aid of the overrun nation because of it. Men will have lost respect for you, and the ambitious among them will seek your downfall and ruin.

It must be understood that the most impressive victory is the one where no force is used. Few will realize anything has happened until it is too late and will usually accept the changes as correct under Heaven. This should be the warlord's main concern. His resources will remain intact and his army will not be tired from unnecessary combat.

If troops are to be used they should be used in a non-combative manner if possible. If you would entirely over-whelm the enemy with manpower, simply surround him by showing your potential power and force. If it becomes necessary to fight, attack with utter resolve in order to divide his resources. Attack from the East and the West; the North and the South. Attack supply lines, attack rest areas—constantly create diversions. The warlord attacks enemy troops directly only when all else has failed and he has properly and adequately provided for the correct placement and efficient use of his own men.

If you do not have sufficient manpower to overrun him with ease, then you must divide him against his own internal alliances. Create discord and disharmony by sending false messages and making false promises to the people. Constantly show the enemy's common people that you are working under the direction of Heaven for their greatest good. Make the enemy's people sympathetic to your cause. To do this you must be exceptional.

If you are equally matched in strength, then you must be the superior commander and beat the enemy with proper strategy based on conviction and application of your own skills. Use the tactics of absolute belief in your need for conquest.

If you are unable to match him in strength, and you have no alternative but to fight, then be sure you have an escape route. If not, you will leave many of your troops dead on foreign soil.

Should you find yourself in an untenable situation, you must immediately withdraw and deal with the consequences. If you are in this situation, you did not plan thoroughly. Get out and either go home or restructure your plans with more authority and conviction prior to making another attack. Regardless, the enemy will now know you and be able to beat you, perhaps easily; this time with possibly more authority and vigor.

These are some of the ways in which a warlord can bring destruction to his own army. Outward appearances of failure may differ in respect to your personal goals, but they are all based on a lack of foresight and planning.

1) Knowing when to attack and not doing so, or knowing not to and forcing the issue.

2) Causing an unnecessary retreat by not correctly employing resources.

3) Not considering the needs of the troops.

4) Constantly changing orders without logical reason.

It is essential that your troops have peace of mind. This is done by properly filling their bellies and rewarding them when they have performed bravely. It implies that you know what they want with regards to the simple pleasures of life. If you do not give this to them they will seek it elsewhere. Peace of mind is also accomplished by not putting them into unnecessary danger.

A warlord of value and worth pays heed to the advice of his ruler, and only after careful consideration should he give orders to his generals. When the ruler is not directly involved with the combat, he will not be aware of the actual conditions of the battle and should not issue orders that would make the generals think the warlord is being usurped. The generals will become confused and possibly rebellious. If the ruler does not understand the means by which warlords exercise responsibility, the officers will see a breakdown in the chain of command. Correct procedure and protocol must be maintained. It is the warlord's responsibility to ensure this.

It is absolutely essential that the warlord not permit the ruler to override his authority. This must be handled delicately because, although the warlord may control the well-being of the entire realm, the ruler owns it. Wisely, he permits the ruler to effect changes of circumstances but does not permit him to speak to the generals. He maintains control of the realm, the ruler, and the ruled.

The ruler must permit the warlord to administer the army and to maintain the overall protection of the empire. Rulers know that intelligent warlords can control and direct the generals, usually at will. If the warlord is usurped by the ruler, rebellion is at hand. To usurp his authority increases the chances for a coup and a wise ruler will see this. If he wishes to overthrow the authority of his warlord, it must be done with stealth and craft.

An astute warlord will recognize an overthrow attempt and stop it before it gets out of hand, at which time he must take control of the entire realm, deposing the ruler if necessary. Betrayal is unacceptable at any level of intent, and in the case of rulers, it will result in the overthrow of the government. The ruler will find himself without troops to defend his position.

Judicious warlords know the methods of maintaining authority and predicting victory in battle. They know when to fight and when not to fight; they know when conditions are correct for the successful engagement of combat. Supplies are in place and the men are enthused. Alert warlords understand the correct deployment of large and small forces, and by this wisdom they see where a small force can overwhelm a large force and when a large force cannot conquer a small force.

Respected warlords maintain high morale among the troops. Without morale there will be dissension and the reason for fighting may not be strong enough to unify the warriors.

Successful warlords are able to lie in wait for an enemy who is not prepared for battle beyond boasting of his ability. He does not attack just to prove he is in control of the situation. He understands the conditions for battle, which include the optimum use of resources. He sees the strengths and weaknesses of the enemy. He also sees the strengths and weaknesses of his own command.

The insightful warlord has trust and faith in his generals. He permits them to express their authority under the right conditions and sees to it that they are rewarded when successful and admonished when they fail because of poor planning. He knows the enemy and himself in order to avoid peril. Because of this knowledge, he will succeed in the field and the administration of the state. If he is unaware of the enemy's strengths but is aware of himself, his chances of victory are evenly matched. If he doesn't know himself and doesn't know the enemy, he is certain to entertain defeat. The ruler should never have picked this man to lead; he is not strong either.

BOOK 4

How to Think of War

*I*n ancient days warriors made themselves unbeatable by
constant practice. Knowing they could never become
invincible, their efforts enabled them to see the vulnerability of intended victims. They did not think in terms of beat-
ing the enemy by overwhelming him with boastful actions,
but rather, they saw the reality of extending their skills
through the enemy, which they acknowledged was the same
thing as physical combat. They were also aware of their own
limitations.

They constantly practiced, knowing there was no other
way they could make the enemy vulnerable. The enemy had
to do that himself. Because a warlord knew how to win does
not mean that he did—but he did know that the enemy had
the same attitudes and would be seeking the same results.
Regardless, he continued to practice until he became the
very object he was seeking and, in so doing, learned that if
invincibility exists at all it lies in the attitude of attack—
offensive or defensive.

To properly defend, the attitude must be that of a thorough attack. To depend strictly upon defense means that
there is not enough strength of purpose in your heart. To

gain victory you must be assured of yourself and attack with all your heart.

Warlords who have mastered defense attack from hidden places and assure their own success. They know when, where, and how to make an attack while defending their positions at the same time. These men of high perception rely on obstacles they have set up for the enemy. In understanding the attack mentality they never permit the enemy to know where the attack is coming from. They attack like lightning and are relentless in their purpose until they have beaten the enemy or have been thrown out of the land. They take no prisoners and do not expect to be spared themselves.

Warlords do not see war as an extension of court etiquette. Men of worth see victory where most men see nothing. They see victory in creating difficulty for the enemy. They foresee victory when the enemy cannot overcome his own inadequacy. This is the only reason for the warlord's existence. If the warlord has visions different from this, then he leads in title only and will accomplish nothing. It is imperative to lead for the people and not for yourself. The people will praise you when they realize the greatness of your actions.

The warlord creates situations where his troops can perish if they fail. He does not let them know he is doing this and is sure to keep their best interests in his own heart. He is always in the same place he sends his men. He ignores the generals' outcries and maintains his conviction and authority. The troops may be frightened, but they follow him if they feel he loves them.

If you understand the needs of warriors and proceed in this fashion, you will be successful; if you don't, you will fail. In acts of desperation, troops will fight as if possessed—they will see no alternative but to succeed or perish.

Ancient warlords always beat the enemy when it was easy to do so because they planned properly and foresaw victory. They did not gain recognition as masters of war during the act of conflict. They knew not to fight when it was difficult, for that would have been foolish and cost them greatly in terms of men and resources, even if the battle was won. They would have lost the respect and confidence of their men. It is always best to permit the enemy to defeat himself with little effort on your part. You should encourage him to destroy himself. You must be very subtle in this attitude in order to reap the rewards of the enemy's overconfidence. Make sure of his ineptitude by understanding the initial attack mentality. The heroic warlord knows when and where to position his troops for maximum effect and least effort. Be a warlord with vision.

Those skilled in the arts of war permit the Spirit of the Heavens to flow within and without themselves. They do not try to coerce Heaven into thinking in their own favor but seek to do that which they believe and accept to be the correct action of Heaven. The wise and great warlord never goes against Heaven's decrees. Heaven makes itself obvious to the man of wisdom.

When the seed of endeavor is planted with authority and conviction, Heaven will instruct him in the proper behavior to gain his desires. Heaven does not move when the man of wisdom wants it to move; he must reflect upon his attitudes and positions in life to see if there is some more appropriate action and intent to be gained through further reflection. If he can think of no other plan of action and truly believes that his cause is just, Heaven, by its very nature, will see his truth and will rush to bring about his dream. This is the nature of the universe. It has no choice but to cooperate with a man of true belief. He always keeps in mind the requirements for success in any endeavor.

This attitude permits the Heavens to see more clearly into the warlord's true desire. He will have shown the proper respect to the Heavens by knowing the virtues of a noble. He is aware of the distance to be traveled on earth and in Heaven if victory is to be attained. He knows how far he must travel and knows how far his troops must carry his desire. He loves them openly and cares for their needs. He knows the value of the supplies to be carried into battle and those that should be left behind as reserves if Heaven should turn aside from his favor. His calculations of manpower are estimated by considering the strengths and weaknesses of each warrior's ability. The warlord knows when each man is in proper position and which weapons he can use. He does not make archers of cooks. He considers the costs of battle on all levels. He examines the possibilities of defeat as well as victory. He does not place himself or his men in positions of needless danger under any circumstances. This is not to be confused with placing troops in positions of peril where they must fight well or die.

When these virtues are understood, his excellence will cause him to emerge victorious from conflict. His armies will revel in glory and see him as a great leader. He will acknowledge their tribute but will not dance in his own light. It is because of his understanding of these things that he will see his men fight with fury, joy, and expectation of victory. As a result of this mentality, the warlord will be respected by his enemies.

Study this significant aspect of the warlord's mentality completely: it contains the genius of accomplishment.

五

BOOK 5

USING THE POWER OF HEAVEN

*I*t is important for the warlord to manage all of his resources by maintaining personal control over them. He may delegate authority in certain respects but is still primarily responsible for his own welfare. It does not matter if there are many affairs to control or if there are few. He manages and controls his own destiny. All is controlled with ease or difficulty depending on his desire, and this will be determined by his understanding of the organization of Heaven.

Management of resources is done by assigning the correct tasks to his staff, with the assurance that those charged are able to accomplish his desires. This is called delegating with intelligence and authority and can only be successful if the warlord knows the capabilities of his men.

He must also know their limitations. A warlord manages his aides in each aspect of his administration. He does not concern himself with the men that his aides command. If the warlord depends on five generals for the completion of the tasks he orders, and those generals have ten captains reporting to them, then the many are controlled by the one through the few. He knows this and uses it to his advantage. The warlord's chiefs can control everything, leaving him free to deal with the further development of the empire, but only if they have been chosen with care and thought to the overall goal of the enterprise. It is essential to maintain this structure—the chain of command—for without it nothing will function harmoniously.

When all is in harmony the army can withstand natural attacks and those that appear to be supernatural. This ability is maintained through correct administration and the proper management of men. When functioning in proper order, an army can make an enemy think that attacks are not what they appear to be. This is reinforced even further if the organization has had proper training and practice. All things that exist have a multitude of variations, some subtle and some not so subtle. With only limited tones in a musical scale and red, blue, and green on the palette, combinations of melodies and colors become infinite. The principles are the same when the warlord administers his court or applies methods to defeating an enemy.

The possibilities are endless under Heaven. That is why each move must be carefully measured and considered. In battle, as everywhere else, combinations of natural and supernatural forces are infinite and cannot be comprehended with ease. The methods to be used are as unfathomable as the ideas that govern existence, and when applied with full force and authority they cannot be stopped. When the warlord is skilled in the ways of war, his attacks are thorough and he is relentless until the goal is achieved. Heaven sees the meaning in his desires and will Itself insist that he attain his goals.

His timing is perfect. His reasoning is perfect. His

resources are perfect. His desires are perfect. All things under Heaven are in accord with his thinking because of his planning for victory. Even so, there is still no guarantee he will succeed if he is only intellectually convinced of victory. He must be convinced of it to the very depths of his soul. Planning is his form of demand, and Heaven, when he is acknowledged by It, will assist to the ends of the universe. The warlord will attain great fortune in war. But if he is not sincere, Heaven will know that too and will not assist him. He will fail and will take down those who believed in him as well.

It must be understood that deceptive actions are significant in war. Organization will indicate if the warlord is entering the place of war with correct action or if he is functioning in chaos. The same attitude of organization will also determine the bravery or cowardice of his men in any circumstance, and their belief will be indicated by right action or weaknesses in battle by the same Heaven that governs the warlord.

When the warlord in strong, he makes the enemy move where and when he wants him to move and keeps him still when he wants him still. Controlling his own destiny, he influences the enemy at will while operating under the providence of Heaven.

A skilled warlord does not depend on his subordinates to wrest victory and profit. Proper planning is what rules the day. With proper organization and intelligent delegation of responsibility he takes control of his destiny. He does not rely on subordinates to explain failure to him. He guarantees his own success by demanding it of himself.

When the warlord has given his heart to preparations for victory, he is not surprised when it comes because his success appears to be divinely guided.

BOOK 6

FORTITUDE AND FRAILTY

The pressures of being a great leader, when they descend onto the shoulders of the mighty warlord, are not understood by lesser men. He is misunderstood, and until his authority is absolute and Heaven has smiled on him, he may be considered mad. It is through his belief in himself, without the support of others to lean on, that he finally does attain greatness: nothing is able to resist him and everything rushes to do his bidding. Because of his belief in this knowledge, he continues on in his quest and does not stop. That is also why Heaven must eventually give way. Heaven provides for all of the following when the warlord has properly considered his actions.

When the warlord is prepared for battle, he is first into the arena of combat and does not shrink because of fear or doubt. His fortitude is fixed and his fighting will be done with ease if he understands the way to achieve his goals. If he arrives late and is insecure in his position, it is because he did not plan properly and can easily be beaten. Wise warlords bring the enemy to them and do not permit the enemy to suck them into false security. He does not permit the alleged power of his enemies to influence him and will always issue the final order: good, bad, or indifferent.

The astute warlord brings the enemy to him by offering something of perceived value. Once the enemy is drawn in, it is simple to execute full authority in the destruction of the attacked state. If he makes the enemy look foolish, the people of that state will reconsider their loyalty as well.

The simplest way to humble, humiliate, and debase your enemy is to cut him off from his supplies. If he is mighty and still comes forward, his avenue of escape will be that much more difficult to attain when he cannot rest and resupply his troops: if you have planned your attacks with intelligence it will be so.

The wise warlord makes advances into enemy territory and does so when he is certain there will be no resistance to his moves. He does not seek to tire his own troops. Deception and subterfuge are essential ingredients to a successful campaign. He appears where the enemy does not expect him. He offers things that are of no value to him, regardless of appearance, even if it includes sacrificing men. He defends what he holds by not permitting the enemy to enter into his camp. He protects his lines of supply by maintaining direct contact with his troops. If the enemy should attack the warlord's supply lines, that enemy would find himself cut off and surrounded by a force that he did not expect.

The warlord of consistent skill never leaves traces of where he has been. He is indistinguishable among the many. His plans are well thought out, but are unfathomable to the enemy. He appears where he is not and disappears into the void without a trace and prepares for his next attack.

He advances, penetrating deeply into the soft spot in the

enemy's armor. When he retreats, he does so with such speed as to tire the enemy troops by forcing them into disadvantageous positions of chaotic chasing, leaving behind a force that can still attack the enemy's supplies. He attacks during retreat and employs ultimate deception.

When the warlord does not wish to enter into battle, he suggests a ground where the enemy cannot follow with ease. He never permits the enemy to know where his attack will come from and sacrifices those things that will protect the region of deception when necessary. When defending a position of weakness, he comes from the side or from behind and scourges the enemy even if it appears that he is coming straight on.

When the enemy must protect many places at the same time, he will inevitably leave some of them undermanned and weak, unless he is exceptionally powerful, in which case the alert warlord will recognize it and consider additional planning prior to combat.

Undermanned and weak positions should be swiftly attacked and overrun. The warlord should keep a small contingent there afterwards to maintain control and forewarn him in case of renewed buildup.

The enemy must be attacked in such manner as to force uneven distribution of his troops. In that way the enemy can be divided and conquered with ease. When the enemy is confused by the initial attack, he will be weak if the dispersion of his troops was forced by the warlord's correct action. If the enemy prepares for an attack to his front, his rear will be weak. If he prepares his mountain troops, then his valley troops will be weak. Perceiving this, the warlord considers the strategy being used by the enemy and understands the importance of resolve in the first strike.

A large force cannot necessarily overpower a smaller force. There are times when the few can do battle with the many and be victorious. It is always wise to prepare defenses against an overpowering force. An overpowering force may not be able to maintain its organization and speed because of problems with mobilization and communication. All things must be weighed and all things must be seen in their own light.

If the small force is adequately organized it can wreak havoc upon the slowness of the larger army. These are called hit-and-run tactics. When used efficiently these methods are used to disperse the main forces of the larger army. In matters of defensive strategy, the smaller army must be sure to select the area of combat for the confrontation, otherwise the larger army will simply walk right over them.

By constantly harassing the larger force, a warlord can determine where its strengths and vulnerabilities lie. It is easy for a small group to disrupt a large group when it is done from the inside. A large group, by its very nature, must permit observers to see its strategy—something that eventually becomes a weakness.

A clever warlord never repeats his successful actions in the same manner. Variations in the universe are infinite, and so are the methods to be used in any actions. In time, a repeated strategy will be learned by the opposition, and they will be able to prepare defenses against it. If new methods of attack do not work after a second attempt, they must be reevaluated.

The warlord must have an alternative method at the ready. Wise warlords always diversify their attacks when necessary.

An army must always remain fluid if it is to flow in the direction of Heaven's way. Without this ability, it becomes less resilient and can be trapped by its own attempts at deception.

In war there are no constants. That is why the variations of Heaven must be accepted and change is made when change is required. Change should also be considered when it is not required and kept in the event of contingencies. Failure to see new ways to do things causes sloppiness in thinking and over-confidence in physical bearing. Avoid this!

In all things there is change. In the seasons, in the days, in the shapes of the moon, and in the fortunes of men. Gain victory with courage and protect your empire with changes in attitudes and constant study to further develop your own desires. The virtuous warlord recognizes this truth and acts on it.

BOOK 7

Manipulation of Circumstance

*T*he warlord with vision understands the ruler's desires
for the future. He maintains the army in accordance
with the knowledge that he will in time be called upon to
protect the empire when the ruler desires expansion. Because
of this, the army is always kept in harmony with the Heavens.
The generals maintain the organization of it through the
chain of command, because they are told of the ruler's desires
by the warlord. Even so, it is difficult to maintain control,
regardless of how organized things may appear to be. Things
will seem difficult when simple and simple when difficult.
The intelligent understand this and maintain control through
manipulation.

Manipulation must be employed as deception/no–deception. This means that there is no predisposed attitude towards
the manipulation of circumstance. Deception/no deception
means you proceed without preconceived notions of victory
or defeat. This is accomplished by proper planning. To create
difficulties along the way for the enemy is to understand this
principle. Even when starting out after a long delay, the warlord who understands this principle arrives before the enemy.

The dangers in any form of manipulation are evident as
are the advantages. Because of this, the wise warlord will not

permit his entire army to chase an objective. He always maintains reserves should the need become evident.

If the warlord acts without wisdom, if he insists his troops move at an unnatural pace, if he leaves behind important equipment and supplies—he does not understand the principles of manipulation. He will fail.

His thinking is erroneous if the objective is caught too quickly and the supplies necessary to fulfill the obligations of the act are not available. He will fail.

If slower moving supplies are unable to get to the main fighting force in time of need or if the troops guarding them are attacked, reinforcements might never reach the front. Here too, he will fail.

These things are the result of incorrect planning and are known as operating with one's feet firmly planted in the air.

If a warlord must move quickly and for any reason leaves some of his supplies unprotected, he did not plan correctly. It is perhaps because the Heavens see fit to bring about disgrace to him. Regardless, he must have access to his rear troops and his supplies. In the same way, he must send scouts ahead to learn the conditions of the country that he is invading. He never enters a foreign country without as much information as he can get. To do so is extremely foolish. It is called having one's head in the clouds.

In order to fully understand the conditions of the state being considered for siege, he employs the devious and unworthy men living in that land. They abound in multitude and will sell their souls for a sense of security under the new masters. They will offer information for fees or favors. This information must be checked to see that it is accurate and to prevent falling into a devious trap. If the information proves to be valid the informer must be rewarded. If the information is false the informer should be disposed of as a warning to others. The information must enable better use of deception/no-deception, otherwise it is meaningless.

Warlords of intent and courage always seek to change conditions of war by dispersal of enemy troops in unorthodox ways—creating conditions that the enemy must deal with to ensure his own safety. This will tire the enemy troops and they will lose heart if they are being used for anything other than warfare.

When manipulating enemy troops, the warlord must understand the principles of action and inaction. When troops must move fast, it is required that the entire contingent move quickly and without delay. This does not mean they rush ahead. The entire organization must be prepared to move with expediency in order to attain the goals and not be tired from the labors of the march.

In times when the army moves slowly, it must appear to the enemy to be majestic in its countenance. Trumpets must blast and drums must beat. The appearance must be of great strength and purpose. The peasants of the country being invaded must report to their superiors and overlords that the approaching army is powerful and that they are frightened. This will cause consternation among the enemy and can be used to cause additional chaos. A general who cannot elicit these responses from the warlord's troops must be replaced immediately with someone who can.

During times of raids and the taking of booty, invading troops must be made to move with purpose and haste. Plundering a country has a tendency to make the invading troops lax in their vigil. If this mentality is permitted, they will become more impressed with the accumulation of trinkets and forget their reason for being there in the first place. The wise warlord must insist that the army gets in and gets out quickly. He knows to take what he can carry with ease, leaving the rest for the people. Otherwise the hatred of the conquered people will travel faster than the wind. Being astute, he does not permit all of his troops to partake in the rape of the conquered land, but shares the booty among all his men. He keeps nothing for himself. His vision must not be for immediate gain but for the future.

When the army stands without motion, it must appear to be massive regardless of manpower. It must function without corruption and the generals must see to this. Men must constantly check their weapons, practice maneuvers, and clean their armor. In this way, reports back to the enemy show poise and conviction of purpose. This too will frighten the enemy troops.

It is important to maintain a system of visual and secret signals consisting of the troops' appearance and communications. The army knows itself through these signals and will respond accordingly when they are received. If there is no system of secret communications, brave warriors may move into battle without assistance. These signals also prevent the cowardly from retreating in the face of battle because they are easily recognizable.

Shouts and yells in battle do much to increase the passion
nd virtue of a warrior. There should be encouragement to
hout in practice and on the field of mortal combat. Favorite
shouts and yells should be made into battle songs to instill
courage.

Uniforms for separate groups may look different from
each other but medals and rank insignia must be the same.
Uniforms must contain one significant symbol that unites
them all. Uniforms should be decorated with signs of bravery.
Medals must be given to those deserving them and must make
a warrior's uniform stand out without being garish. These
medals should suggest a mystique so that those without them
will want to have them as well. This will increase their desire
to show more courage and excellence in battle. Bravery is
bravery and is not to be considered differently by different
troops. Recognition and reward must be equal. If it is not, the
warlord may find himself surrounded by troops who do not
share an understanding of value. This will cause loss of
morale. Unhappy and confused men do not fight bravely.

The warlord must appreciate his troops' desire to be
home instead of on the field of battle, so he will divide them
into smaller groups, enabling them to maintain their own
identity without becoming melancholy. These smaller units
stay to themselves during bivouac but join a greater force in
time of battle. The warlord employs this idea knowing that
troops will maintain their image and vie with one another to
do a better job.

The spirits of most warriors, with rare exception, vary
with time. In the morning a warrior is filled with vitality and

seeks to do battle, in the afternoon he may tire if the expectancy of combat has not been fulfilled, and in the evening he will long for home and seek to be there instead of being on the field of battle.

It is incumbent upon the warlord to see that his troops are constantly employed. In long campaigns, troops will eventually lose heart if they are not kept busy. If the troops' minds are not busy then they will devise additional ways of not doing their duty. They will have to be punished. Resources and time will have been wasted in winning control over them again.

The wise warlord understands that his men will be ready to fight at any given time if they are constantly aware of the conditions around them. The troops must be told their tasks are important, even when they think the tasks are meaningless. This is part of manipulation by deception/no-deception. If troops have their minds occupied with even the slightest tasks and their bellies are not overfilled, they do not lag behind without enthusiasm. They will wait in harmony and peace until the time comes for them to fight with valor for victory, the ruler, and themselves.

When warriors are serene and confident in their leader's abilities, they will fight with ferocity, unaware of the fear of combat. They will not be intimidated by the enemy's appearance. They will prove worthy of reward.

Successful warlords never attack an enemy's elite troops. They are called "elite" by their own leaders because they are considered to be above common warriors in heart and skill. To fight them in the open is asking for trouble. Your own elite troops are to be used only when situations call for it and at no other time. It is purposeless for a chicken to fight a snake. It is wise to hold elite contingents in reserve, using them mostly to protect the realm and the ruler's house.

Never attack if you see the enemy in prime condition and if his appearance is strong and steady. His organization may be stronger than yours and you will need to replan your strategy.

Do not attack the enemy if he holds high ground. Gravity does not work upwards. It is important to consider your resources when this type of battle in indicated. Never attack the enemy when his back is against a barrier of retreat. He will fight with desperation and inflict serious damage if he sees no way out.

If he pretends to retreat, do not follow him until you see his entire army moving away from you. Never permit offerings of deception to force you into combat based on your overconfidence.

If you encounter the enemy on his march home, do not attack. He is leaving and has submitted to you. If you attack him when he is in retreat, he will have no alternative but to die for his honor. This type of warrior is exceedingly dangerous.

If you surround the enemy, you must see that he has an avenue of escape. If you press the enemy when he is trying to leave the area of battle, he will fight with desperation and you will encounter great loss, regardless of your organization.

Understand these principles well. They are the foundation of proper and intelligent manipulation of troops.

BOOK 8

Variations of Reality in War

*T*here are variations in all strategies and tactics. Understanding the varieties of things is necessary for the warlord of worth to be able to intelligently manipulate his troops
regardless of prevailing conditions. To function successfully,
the possibility of variations occurring either in part or in total
must be in the mind of the proficient administrator.

One of the most important variations to consider is the
resting place for troops. Warlords must insure that they are
never caught in an area where they can be taken by surprise.
It is difficult to do this when troops are in a place of general
mobility. If troops are dispersed over too broad an area, signals
will be difficult to pass. Communications must be ongoing at
all times, and there can be no breakdown if the warlord's
orders are to be acted upon with immediacy during any
aspect of the campaign.

In time of war, troops should be encamped in a place of
complete safety, but they must not be permitted to become
complacent and, as a result, derelict in their duties. If they are
encamped where their safety may be at risk, they will maintain resourcefulness and be vigilant towards intrusions. When
surrounded by enemies they know they have to fight to sur-
vive. It will keep them alert.

Knowing about matters such as this is one thing: understanding when and where to act upon them is another. Regardless of how things seem, there are some places—mentally and physically—that must not be entered into until proper control of thought develops proper strategy. It is the wise warlord who knows when it is appropriate to fight and when it is far more effective to leave the area without a contest, still emerging victoriously in the end.

Because of the variations and the uncertainties of circumstance, there are times when the warlord must disobey the commands of the ruler. The mentality of conquest is subtle, and before disobeying an order a warlord must have a deep understanding of the ruler's prime directive. To disobey because it may appear fashionable can only result in chaos. If the warlord is strong and the ruler has assigned responsibility to him, but suddenly changes directives in the middle of a campaign, there may be something happening that the warlord is unaware of. A prudent warlord is always apprised of changes in condition. He creates them. Disobeying a ruler's directive can lead to an overthrow of the entire chain of command, resulting in a military coup. Officers who disobey without just cause must be put to death as an example, unless they can justify their act. Should this ever happen, the contemplative warlord must carefully examine all avenues of cause and effect to understand the reasons for it and to ensure that it never happens again.

The warlord who truly knows his troops and the directives of the ruler can act on his own, if it is for the benefit of the entire state. When an order is issued it must be followed without question. If a general acts through his own volition and without authorization, then he must be punished, regardless of the outcome of his actions. If the warlord does not punish violators under these circumstances, he is seeking to indulge his troops: they will eventually rebel. The warlord must rule with an iron fist and not necessarily in a velvet glove.

The quickest route may not be the shortest. The most difficult terrain to overcome may not be the most disadvantageous. It is not wise to capture territory if it will prove difficult to hold. Breakdowns in communication can place an otherwise victorious warlord in an area unreachable by reinforcements. The dangers inherent in a military expedition must be carefully weighed. The troops are never jeopardized, regardless of the ruler's orders.

There is no way for specific circumstance to be foretold. The intelligent warlord carefully examines his own methods prior to attacking. He is able to see the advantages of his immediate plans and the inherent dangers as well. By manipulating the conditions of his plan, he can overcome obstacles that he discovers when initiating the primary attack. By doing these things the fates will smile upon him.

If the warlord wins the war without combat, it is because he is a master of deception and guile. He can do this by presenting gifts to his enemy and causing confusion among the enemy ranks by taking their attention from the matter at hand. He uses things certain to have the effect he wants, such as intoxicating beverages, beautiful women, and expensive gifts that would whittle down enemy resources should they seek to duplicate them.

He also uses cunning to deceive and manipulate the ministers of the enemy state by finding delicate matters to blackmail them with. There are always numerous methods that make themselves available to the shrewd warlord in the execution of his desires to fulfill the needs of his goals.

A fierce warlord must never question his own morality. If he does, he is more concerned with popular opinion than he is with command and is not fierce. Heaven will not help him maintain his control and position. He must never let his guard down and must understand that those who do combat with words will still rely on his skills in the field should they fail in their diplomatic attempts.

The true warlord never lets his sword be out of reach. He keeps it close because he is aware of the calamities that can destroy him: imprudence, cowardice, belligerence, arrogance, and charity.

If he is imprudent, he will think in terms of foolish behavior to gain his goals. Cowardly acts will cause him to lose his control and, in time, his life. Belligerence and bullnosed bravado will constantly force people to challenge him, until someone succeeds in overthrowing his authority. Arrogance will not permit him to see an issue unfolding about him. Charity and overbearing compassion will show him as a sniveler. Bad attitudes bring death to a person believing he is unbeatable.

The wise warlord tests anyone he thinks should be a general and protector of the state. Many tests must be given on a continuous basis. It is curious that rulers do not see fit to test their commanders completely before giving them the responsibility of the nation. As a result, many nations have been dismantled.

九

BOOK 9

THE VIRTUE OF CHANGING POSITIONS

*T*he man who would be warlord knows of the inevitability of change in the administrative practice of maintenance of the state. This may occur many times during periods of growth and development. Being resilient is a virtue of the warlord with vision, and knowing how change functions in the management of a state is essential. Without it there is decay and loss of the society.

When a conflict is completed, the warlord should be in the position of controlling the state from the attitude of a higher viewpoint. By holding to this outlook, it is difficult for anyone to supersede his directives. Aides are easy to control because they are in line to receive orders. Warlords must realize the necessity of preventing aides from acting subversively—openly or not. Many times, a second in command will seek to gain control once the prime objective has been gained.

This is where an overall view is advantageous. Functional administrative duties can then be delegated, results can be seen more clearly, and the warlord's personality will not interfere with the points of view expressed by his aides. His goals are more clearly visualized.

This broader viewpoint creates obstacles for an enemy with evil intentions. The meritorious warlord understands that the best position to be in is the one where difficulty emanates from his own point of view directly into the enemy's vision. This gives the enemy two things to consider: the need to keep his own troops under control and the constant effort needed to get around obstacles that may appear anywhere at any time. A capable warlord employing intelligent deception always seeks ways to confuse all known and potential enemies.

In physical confrontation it is better to have the sun behind your back and in the eyes of the enemy. The enemy is forced to adjust with every move he makes towards you. Attitudes are affected, and disarray will cause the enemy to lose composure and make foolish moves.

When the enemy comes straight on, intent on confrontation, it is wise to permit him to advance with at least half of his troops before responding. The prudent warlord never responds to acts of bravado, knowing them to be false gestures. To initiate a confrontation when the enemy is not completely under your control is to invite defeat because of improper planning and disregard for potential strengths—apparent and unapparent. Never advance your troops into a less than heavenly position. Do not permit the errors of variance to interfere with your attack. This brings about defeat.

It is better to draw the enemy into you by preparing devices that cause him to fall. When drawing the enemy in, be sure to have the sun at your back and the shadows of doubt will fall onto the faces of those approaching you. They will not see clearly and will be more concerned with trying to maintain their calmness before entering battle.

The warlord should always be prepared for dangerous traps and hidden devices that would undermine his advances. Advance scouts should be used to bring back valid intelligence, which the warlord needs if he is to be successful in overcoming any odds by making wise decisions. It does not matter how these decisions are made, as long as he realizes he is the one responsible for the ultimate outcome, regardless of the advice of his aides.

The warlord must be aware of his surroundings at all times. There are always spies lurking and people who would do anything to undermine his advances. Even in his own command there will be men working against him, in ways in which he or even they may not be aware. They may speak out of turn or present a gift to an unknown enemy; therefore warlords do not openly reveal their plans.

When the warlord moves forward he must keep scouts in front to observe the advance territory. He must have scouts in the rear and to all sides in order to head off any potential attack. A constant flow of information is essential for the security and safety of the warlord and his protection of the ruler's desires. He must be sure the information he receives is correct.

When enemy agents talk of peace the warlord must make sure the enemy is under control and not merely scheming. It is important to understand all of the signals used by the enemy. Activity seen where none should be must be investigated immediately to prevent falling into a trap. When the enemy talks of appeasement he may in reality be preparing to attack. When the enemy is suggesting cooperation he may be planning deception.

It is the nature of the implementation of war by deception that the enemy be shown the futility of counter attacking and reclaiming his losses. A warlord must be capable of holding newly gained territory. To win in battle and yet lose in negotiations for the maintenance of peace will cause the people to wonder about his intentions.

There are signals to be understood before a physical attack. It does not matter if negotiations have been fruitful or a waste of time. These signals are used by the enemy both when he has doubts or when he thinks he can entrap an advancing warlord.

If there is clamor in the enemy camp, the enemy may be nervous or may only be suggesting it to an enemy. If there are guests in the camp, the warlord must know if they are planning together. When the enemy sees an advantage and does not rush to take it, he is insecure and his troops will be without heart.

There are countless signals that the thoughtful warlord must recognize if he is to maintain authority and control. If he is not alert to the warnings and advisories of his aides, he is asking Heaven to protect him without adequate preparation.

If rewards, grand dinners, and impressive gifts are given too often by the enemy, he may be trying to maintain harmony, while preparing his troops to attack the advancing army. If a general is rewarding men too freely and punishing with laxity, he may be losing control of his troops. They may not respond when needed.

It is important to recognize what it means when the enemy is boisterous and in high spirits but does not attack. If the enemy continues to conduct business in this manner and does not appear to prepare to leave the area, the warlord must investigate thoroughly and gain mastery of the situation immediately.

The warlord must understand the value in giving orders and expecting them to be followed without question. When orders are given uniformly there will be no worry about them being followed. When the orders are slanted in one direction or another there will be discontent and the troops will consider it to be favoritism. If this continues, the troops will eventually cease to follow orders with enthusiasm and, in time, they may rebel.

When the warlord gives orders with fairness and authority, the expected results will be for the benefit of all concerned, the ruler will be shown respect by the actions of the troops, and all will be in harmony with Heaven. All will prosper.

BOOK 10

CONTROL AND MAINTENANCE
OF TERRITORY

*P*hysical territories, as well as areas of administration, are classified according to their capacity for being controlled. They should all be considered as equal. As with everything else under the Heavens, each has advantages and disadvantages. These places are known as vulnerable, ensnaring, ambivalent, blocked, steep, and too far afield.

1) A place of vulnerability is accessible to both the warlord and his enemies. Maintenance of this territory is advantageous to the owner because it may afford a factor of slight control. An invader is easily seen coming into view. It is always an area of contention and is hardly defensible without mortal combat. It is a place of no permanent control. Seek to avoid this place.

2) Ground that is ensnaring is a place that can easily cause the holder to be caught in his own webs of intrigue, resulting in disaster if it is not vigilantly maintained. It is not a good place to be because the enemy can attack unprepared troops with ease. Even if the troops are prepared, they can still be caught in a place where it would be difficult for them to escape.

3) Ambivalent territory is bad for all parties. It is here that the warlord forces the conditions to draw out half of the enemy army

before entering into a battle. It is a place where no one is in control. Prudence suggests keeping it protected with an unstoppable force, or by complete withdrawal. Fighting to control this place will result in fierce combat with no apparent advantage.

4) Blocked territory suggests that a battle is inevitable because there is no way for either side to maintain control. If the enemy controls this area he must be coerced out of the position before the warlord can ultimately destroy him. If it is controlled by the warlord, his troops must prepare traps and pitfalls for the enemy. An avenue of escape must be maintained.

5) In steep ground the advantage lies with whoever is in the higher position. The enemy has to take an offensive against indeterminate odds because of the requirements to get to the top. If the enemy controls the area, then he must be drawn out, or if that cannot be accomplished with ease, the wise warlord will abandon his plans for the day and rethink his method.

6) Territory managed from far afield creates difficulties in maintenance because defense depends on the distance supplies and men may have to travel. It is difficult to maintain territory from afar and to govern from a distance.

The warlord must learn to manage all types of territory and personnel, making sure that he can negotiate effectively in any circumstance. A land once taken and then lost is twice as difficult to recover. The nature of the territory to be protected must be known to ensure proper management.

Troops should be compared to the types of territory being administered. They are an extension of the state and must be managed with intelligence and understanding. If soldiers are strong and the officers are weak, acts of insubordination, which cannot be tolerated under any instance, will have to be handled.

If officers are strong, the troops will seek to please them. If they are overbearing, the soldiers will lose heart and they will not follow into battle. If the officers are arrogant and they do not consider the needs of the men, the army is in disarray and will not be controlled in battles. If a warlord is weak and without firm morality or if his orders are ambivalent, the officers will not respond properly, the troops will have no leadership, the chain of command will falter, and the needs of the ruler will go unserved. Chaos will result.

If warlords are not kept aware of the conditions of the army, if they are unaware of the need for reinforcements and supplies, they will be seen as not in control and their orders will go unheeded. If they try to overrun a larger force with bravado instead of intelligent planning, they will cause the downfall of their army and any gains they may have previously made will be lost.

Whether his knowledge is acted upon or not, without consideration and understanding the warlord will find that he has caused the needless death of many of his men. The men in his command will come to distrust him and will realize they are not being led with discretion and intelligence. They will rebel.

It is important for the warlord to understand management of newly acquired territory and the proper employment of troops. It is foolish to know the land and not the men. The reverse is true as well. One without the other is incomplete.

In like manner, a man assigned a specific task may not be able to complete it if he does not know what is expected of him. The same applies if he gets where he is sent and has no idea of why he was sent there. To understand unity, meditate on duality.

Warlords would be wise to analyze the conditions of war before entering into it. They would be wise to consider all aspects of an alliance prior to making one. They would be wise to consider the reasons for another's wishing to associate with them. They would be wise to attend to their own needs before entering into agreements. They would be wise to seek council from their generals and rulers. They would be wise to think twice about a request for the assistance of troops and supplies. Then they should make their decisions.

A warlord who considers the needs and desires of others before himself should be praised to Heaven. Such a man is rare and will not permit personal gain to interfere with the performance of his duties. A wise ruler should see that this warlord is given every tool he needs to create the state in the image of the ruler's intentions. His men will follow him. His generals will praise him. The people will listen to him. He will be loved because of the people's fear of his loss.

He may appear to be weak to those without heart and will be a master of deception because he has no deception in his own heart. He administers reward and punishment with the same force and intent. He does not play favorites, regardless of the outcome. He marches with his men when they are marching. He eats only when their food is cooked. He drinks only when they are not thirsty.

He does not coddle them like children. He treats them as he prefers to be treated. He respects them and they respect him. He rules justly and they both love him and fear him. They will do his bidding without question. They will follow him into battle and die for him if necessary.

The troops will do these things because they know their best interests are in their warlord's heart. They will know he has studied the situation completely and will not permit them to be trapped in danger as a result of improper planning. Victory will be resolute and they will all rejoice in the name of the ruler, which is as it should be. They will know their warlord as a true warrior: he has acknowledged them as well.

The warlord gets his reward from the excellent performance of his deeds. He knows that the trappings of his office will bring him the material goods he desires, but he does not concern himself with them. He leads because it is his nature.

BOOK 11

As with all things, there are correct and incorrect methods of doing anything for any reason. All things relating to an action should be well thought-out prior to its beginning. These nine considerations are the fundamental elements of war. They are called dissipation, bordering, coincidence, correspondence, concentration, signification, laboring, entrapment, and the place of death.

Dissipation takes place on home ground when troops are not adequately prepared to defend the state. Dissipation arises from the troops' desire to go home. Fighting should not take place on home ground if it can be avoided. It indicates that proper planning for its avoidance was not strongly considered. If an invading army approaches and was not observed, the troops will seek to protect their individual homes. Because of this, they are on the defensive and are vulnerable. This is not good for the state. The educated warlord knows that when he throws the enemy into a place of dissipation, confusion will result and the enemy will be unable to deploy his forces correctly.

Bordering suggests an attitude of being neither here nor there. When approaching the border of a neighboring land, making a feeble attempt to invade it is disheartening to the troops. They will think there is a possibility of incomplete conviction on the part of the warlord and this may cause them to think about failure. A wise warlord forces the enemy into bordering places to keep him off guard while harassing the enemy troops with deceptive ploys.

Coincidence suggests that Heaven acts according to whim. The wise warlord cannot permit the vagaries of fortune to coerce his focus. It is incorrect for him to do so. Coincidental factors can be controlled by an awareness that the enemy army cannot advance when it is unsure of its strategy, and when the reports they receive are deceptive, forcing them to commit mistakes in judgment.

Correspondence suggests being able to maintain full communications between all of the troops and the capital. The advantage is of being able to build necessary fortifications when and where they are required. When the warlord prevents the enemy from corresponding, normal channels of communications are cut off, and in their place false messages can further disrupt the harmonious functions of the enemy.

The attitude of *concentration* is one of wisdom. Resources are kept intact and they are immediately accessible. This attitude permits the movement of troops and supplies so they are positioned where they are needed, when they are needed. Once a warlord is able to supply his army at will, the goals will be attained with direct and specific results. Victory favors this thinking. Understanding his position relative to the enemy enables the warlord to concentrate his thoughts and actions. He prohibits the enemy from gathering materials for its forces. This can create mass confusion, which can quickly bring about the enemy's downfall—without mortal combat.

Signification means that the warlord has perhaps entered too deeply into a foreign land without adequate reinforcements. He is unable to reinforce his troops because of a lack of understanding of the ground to be covered. Without proper supplies he is only able to pose a potential threat. The enemy is now in a position to destroy him. The position of signification can also mean deception/no-deception and is very useful in keeping the enemy off balance. The enemy is forced to think in terms other than what they are aiming for. This gives a prudent warlord time to maneuver and manipulate all other areas.

Laboring means that maintenance and administration of the place where the warlord is to issue orders from has not been properly protected. This creates an unhappy army because it becomes more concerned with its ability to stay intact and not with its ability to do battle. By creating a place of laboring for the enemy, the warlord keeps the enemy's army from advancing with ease. Instead, it is forced to maintain control of its environment.

A *place of entrapment* is dangerous and the astute warlord must consider avenues of penetration and escape with equal reasoning. It is easy for the enemy to circle and systematically trap the invading army. There will be no easy way to be rid of the dangers, regardless of the skill of the warlord. Entrapment is best done when the enemy escapes from one deception and falls directly into another. All avenues of escape are cut off when entrapment is intelligently employed.

The *place of death* is the worst of all. It can also be the best of all places to be. The warlord who permits himself to be caught in a place of death has not considered all of the conditions, or his leadership is profound. In order to escape this situation the troops must fight out of desperation. If they succeed, they may lose the desire to fight again and express themselves through insubordination.

The place of death must be carefully calculated. Leaders must properly deploy their men or an attitude of failure will descend upon them. Wise warlords use this condition to their advantage. When troops find themselves in the place of death, they will fight without thought. They will fight to protect each other. They will be terrified and they will become demons. They will fight for the glory of the fight itself. When they know they are in this place of death, they will also know they have nothing to lose and will fight with passion. If they win they go home, if they fail they die. There is no middle ground in a place of death.

It is essential for the enlightened warlord to understand the differences in these nine places of mind and body. Great care should be given to the planning for all possibilities when entering into conflict. All possibilities exist—known and unknown—and should be considered as part of the overall plan so that snap decisions in the field will not cost too much in men, materials, time, and effort.

The great warlord provides for reality with his understanding of deception/no-deception and does not permit his reasoning to fail him. He is always serene and calm. He never divulges his plans to his subordinates until the orders are given. His men must never think as he does. If they are permitted to think along with him, they will determine that there is no need for his leadership. He does not let his men talk among themselves about things that can frighten them. He constantly changes his plans and methods of administration. By constantly changing rest areas he keeps them alert to possible attack from unknown areas. No one knows what he is doing. He constantly changes routes to battlefields. He leads his men deep into enemy territory and does not abandon them. He cuts off areas of retreat and leads them to places of death once he is convinced his plans will work and he has laid the proper groundwork for its execution. He deceives his allies when they want him to go before them. Constantly creating difficulty for the enemy, he breaks down their morale. He uses false approaches and creates false attitudes of overconfidence. When he is ready to attack, he does so with utter conviction and expectation of victory. His troops follow without question.

The superb warlord does not hesitate to take advantage of a favorable circumstance with which Heaven has presented him. He is lenient but does not permit compassion to cause him to become indulgent. He moves and strikes like a poisonous snake, sinking his fangs deeply into the enemy, bringing about the enemy's downfall and subjugation. This is the mark of an enlightened warlord.

BOOK 12

Fierceness in Combat

Fierceness is essential in mortal combat. It is never dependent on the amount of destruction you wish to bring upon the enemy. There must be no hesitancy in using any method to bring about the complete and utter destruction of the enemy. It is the only way to ensure victory of a lasting nature.

Fierceness is a natural state when troops see the wisdom of their leader. Correct tactics are required to ensure that any approach to the enemy will be consistent with victory. It is the perceptive warlord who prepares for any eventuality and accepts victory with a glad heart. To do battle and be saddened by it is not to be considered meritorious. A warlord and his warriors exist to maintain the state for the ruler.

If the warlord is also the ruler, then it is advantageous for him to understand the need for the destruction of the leaders he is overthrowing. He should be sage and think of nothing except victory, followed by proper and intelligent maintenance of the conquest. When this is done, all things under Heaven respond with harmony in accordance with his true desires.

All supplies and materials for the invasion should be on hand at all times. It is a time of laboring when the warlord must seek weapons in order to repel an attack. Likewise, he must have adequate resources available if he is to take the offensive.

He must know that timing is essential for victory and must be in accord with Heaven before starting an offensive or defensive attack. Both conditions are the same in the eyes of the warlord.

When the attack is begun the warlord makes sure that his timing is correct with regard to all conditions. If the attack is easily repelled, then it is not wise to attempt another entrance into the enemy camp without reconsidering the situation. The enemy may now be prepared and will deal destruction in return for entrance into their domain. They will be merciless. Restructure the components of the attack and create more difficulty before entering enemy ground a second time. If you are repelled a second time it is prudent to get out entirely.

The warlord understands the types of attack to be used. If an attack is begun from the outside of the enemy camp and produces the results sought after, it may not be necessary to enter into the midst of the enemy. Perhaps the enemy will destroy himself by being unprepared. If you enter into the enemy camp be prepared to fight furiously and make sacrifices where necessary. The enemy is fighting from a place of death.

Let your attack be of such ferocity as to destroy the morale of the enemy. Attack his lines of supply. Use your engineers to destroy his machinery and equipment for survival. Destroy his records and sources of information. Use any method you can devise to accomplish these ends. Be merciless.

Any other form of thinking is incorrect and Heaven will not favor you if you show leniency where none is required. Compassion incorrectly placed will not bring victory; it will bring humiliation regardless of the outcome of the battle. Too many people will have discriminate thoughts about your actions, and it will cost you respect in the eyes of your superiors and your men.

The ruler regards the warlord as the protector of the realm. You must be merciless or someone of more resolve will eventually challenge your authority. Your best warriors must be aware of your total commitment. They will know that should they consider a rebellion they will find themselves up against stone fortifications. If they are foolish enough to try and they fail, they must be dealt with in an appropriate fashion.

The adroit warlord constantly redefines his own principles of war. When he is not in danger he does not fight if he can use alternate methods to destroy the enemy. He does not fail to exploit his victory without delay. He does not act in regard to his own desires but acts for the betterment of the people, the state, and the ruler. Never losing his calmness and poise, he always appears to be serene.

Anger prevents even the greatest of leaders from acting intelligently. Rage and passion are not substitutes for cold-blooded planning in the destruction of an enemy. The judicious warlord understands all of this and maintains his position with respect to Heaven. Heaven looks upon him with approval as a leader of good cause. He is favored among all others. The state is maintained in joy and the ruler is able to relax while making further preparations for the future with confidence.

BOOK 13

Spies and Traitors

*I*t is important for the warlord to have information coming from all corners of the realm. Some of the information he receives will be good and useful. Other information
will lie in the realm of deception/no-deception.

When the ruler is preparing for war, the expense of run-
ning the state can become excessive. It is essential that information be useful and not costly due to the implementation of
mistakes.

If a warlord fights battles that last for extended periods of
time and does not use the resources available to him for victory, then he is wasting those resources by not using them and
does not have the goals of the ruler in his heart. He expends
effort and energy needlessly by not seeking assistance which
can make him more effective and his victory quicker.

Stalemates in battle are caused by a lack of information
and supplies. The wise warlord knows that to beat the enemy
he must have information that he can use to win. He must
also be aware of receiving too much information. This is as
bad as not receiving enough information and can confuse
matters, making it difficult to initiate correct action from wise
decisions.

An efficient warlord is discerning. He realizes he cannot get special information by petitioning the gods nor can it be gotten by ordaining soothsayers and priests. This information can only be gotten from men who will do what is necessary for their own causes. They are called spies and traitors.

There are many types of spies and their differences must be known. Proper usage of their skills is also advantageous. If they are available, and the intelligent warlord knows who they are and does not use them, then perhaps someone with a more astute vision of the world will. There are five different types of spies. They are called foreign, internal, counter, extraneous, and vital. They are all to be thought of as secret agents and are as deadly as vipers. This must be realized.

Agents are invaluable and must be treated accordingly when they provide information that can foster victory. They must never be taken for granted, and their identity must never be revealed. If they are found out, they are certain to be put to death by the enemy. This reason alone suggests the potential value of their information. Their worth can never be estimated.

A foreign agent is a spy who comes to the warlord from the enemy country. He is a citizen and is usually displeased with conditions. He may not have connections into the government but he can relate the true feelings of the people of his native land.

Internal agents are those who are working for the government of the enemy and are displeased with national conditions and their own lots in life. They will sell information to the highest bidder. They have no loyalty to anyone, and though their information may appear to be valuable, it must be thoroughly checked. Living life through a façade, they are self-serving and have no values other than their own. They do not care who is victorious.

Counteragents are internal spies who have been found out, and rather than being put to death, they act with treason to save their lives. The wise warlord tempers them with lavish gifts, turning them to his own cause. They must be handled gently and given the latitude they need to operate. Care must be taken to determine that they are not planted double agents. This can be learned by observing their activities and conduct. It should be realized that they may be aspects of the enemy's deception/no-deception attitudes.

Extraneous agents are those in the warlord's employ who are untrustworthy. They are constantly given erroneous information knowing that they are working as double spies for the enemy in like manner to a counteragent. Dispose of them when they have served their purposes to prevent them from turning on you.

Vital secret agents are natural citizens of the warlord's realm who devote their lives to the propagation of the ruler's desires. They enter into foreign countries and return with information. Their mentality does not permit them to turn into extraneous agents. They are true to the cause: their main concern being the ruler and the people. They are usually very intelligent and deceive the enemy because of their outward appearances.

All information is gotten from other people, so whatever their motivation, they are spies. All governments and all businesses are infested with spies of every type. Sometimes the spies themselves do not know they are spies. The judicious

warlord is careful in selecting the men with whom he sur-
rounds himself.

In matters of working with agents of any type, it is essential that the warlord be just and compassionate in these matters. He must also be subtle to elicit the information in the
spirit it is intended to be used. All agents, regardless of their
position and rank, should be disposed of immediately if they
cause the slightest concern regarding their truth and devotion.

When the warlord is preparing to enter into battle with
an enemy he must know the names of the enemy commanders, the size of the enemy army, and the positions they use
to bivouac. Without this information he is as a blind and deaf
person entering into a perilous journey. Secret agents will get
this information for him. Understanding the mentality of
agents is important when recruiting them. Information
gleaned from native and internal spies gives the warlord the
power needed to employ deception/no-deception tech-
niques and methods.

Everyone has their place and everyone has their value.
This perception permits the intelligent use of agents. Most of
the information is gotten from the double agent. Counteragents will provide you with additional spies when they are
needed—native and internal. The vital agent, incalculable in
value, is too nearsighted.

Agents are of the utmost importance to the successful
operations of the warlord. Only those warlords who are intelligent and enlightened can use them properly. Without secret
operations, a war is a meaningless act of gratuitous violence

that does nothing except destroy all the people and all the resources.

Study these lessons well. To master them means you understand the true arts of war.

ABOUT THE AUTHOR

Stephen F. Kaufman, Hanshi, 10th Dan

An acknowledged Founding Father of American Karate, Hanshi Kaufman originally trained on Okinawa in the 1950s and has held the title of Hanshi since 1991. He is the founder of Hebi-ryu karate do: Dojo no Hebi, School of the Snake. He has taught for military organizations, law enforcement agencies, and many community centers and public agencies. Hanshi lectures and teaches strategy and motivation throughout the world.

He is the author of many books, including *Musashi's Book of Five Rings, Sun Tzu's Art of War, The Shogun Scrolls, The Living Tao* and *Zen and the Art of Stickfighting*. His latest works, *Sword in the Boardroom* and *Formal Hebi-ryu Combat Karate Studies*, are soon to be released. Hanshi's books have been translated into many languages.

Hanshi can be contacted at PO Box 135, Lenox Sta., NYC, NY 10021 or email: hanshi@hanshi.com. His websites are www.hanshi.com and www.hanshi.com/seminar.

The Tuttle Story:
"Books to Span the East and West"

Many people are surprised to learn that the world's leading publisher of books on Asia had humble beginnings in the tiny American state of Vermont. The company's founder, Charles E. Tuttle, belonged to a New England family steeped in publishing.

Tuttle's father was a noted antiquarian book dealer in Rutland, Vermont. Young Charles honed his knowledge of the trade working in the family bookstore, and later in the rare books section of Columbia University Library. His passion for beautiful books—old and new—never wavered throughout his long career as a bookseller and publisher.

After graduating from Harvard, Tuttle enlisted in the military and in 1945 was sent to Tokyo to work on General Douglas MacArthur's staff. He was tasked with helping to revive the Japanese publishing industry, which had been utterly devastated by the war. When his tour of duty was completed, he left the military, married a talented and beautiful singer, Reiko Chiba, and in 1948 began several successful business ventures.

To his astonishment, Tuttle discovered that postwar Tokyo was actually a book-lover's paradise. He befriended dealers in the Kanda district and began supplying rare Japanese editions to American libraries. He also imported American books to sell to the thousands of GIs stationed in Japan. By 1949, Tuttle's business was thriving, and he opened Tokyo's very first English-language bookstore in the Takashimaya Department Store in Nihonbashi, to great success. Two years later, he began publishing books to fulfill the growing interest of foreigners in all things Asian.

Though a westerner, Tuttle was hugely instrumental in bringing a knowledge of Japan and Asia to a world hungry for information about the East. By the time of his death in 1993, he had published over 6,000 books on Asian culture, history and art—a legacy honored by Emperor Hirohito in 1983 with the "Order of the Sacred Treasure," the highest honor Japan can bestow upon a non-Japanese.

The Tuttle company today maintains an active backlist of some 1,500 titles, many of which have been continuously in print since the 1950s and 1960s—a great testament to Charles Tuttle's skill as a publisher. More than 60 years after its founding, Tuttle Publishing is more active today than at any time in its history, still inspired by Charles Tuttle's core mission—to publish fine books to span the East and West and provide a greater understanding of each.